THE INDIAN STREET PERFORMANCES

A CULTURAL EXPLORATION OF INDIA'S STREET PERFORMANCES

DR. JAGADEESH PILLAI

|| Dedicated to all wisdom seekers around the world ||

℘

Contents

Contents

Prayer

**"Om Bhadram Karnebhih Shrunuyaama
DevaahBhadram Pashyemaakshabhiryajatraah
SthirairangaistushtuvaamsastanoobhihVyashema
Devahitam YadaayuhSwasti Na Indro
VridhashravaahSwasti Nah Pooshaa
VishwavedaahSwasti Nastaarkshyo ArishtanemihSwasti
No Brihaspatir DadhaatuOm Shantih, Shantih, Shantih"**

The literal meaning of this mantra is: OM. O Gods! Let us
hear auspicious words from our ears. O reverent Gods! Let
us behold propitious visions from our eyes, let our organs
and body be stable, healthy, and strong. Let us do that
which is pleasing to the gods in the life span allotted to us.
May Indra, inscribed in the scriptures, bring us fortune!
May Pushan, the knower of the world, grant us prosperity!
May Trakshya, who vanquishes enemies, bestow us with
blessings! May Brihaspati bring us success!
OM Peace, Peace, Peace.

About The Author

Dr. Jagadeesh Pillai is a renowned Guinness World Record holder, writer, and researcher hailing from Varanasi, also known as the abode of Lord Shiva. With a Ph.D. in Vedic Science and a range of creative ideas and achievements, he is a true polymath. He is the author of more than 100 books including Research Publications. Although his roots can be traced back to Kerala, the people of Varanasi hold him in high regard and affectionately consider him one of their own.

In 1998, Dr. Pillai was offered a job at Banaras Hindu University, but he left the position after only two months to pursue greater goals in life. He believed that in order to study Indian scriptures and engage in other creative endeavours, he needed to retire from the daily grind of working solely for money at a young age.

He started an export business from scratch, using the knowledge he had gained from a previous job in the industry. His intelligence and unique approach to business led to great success in a short period of time, earning him more in just a decade and a half than he would have in a lifetime working in a government job. Upon the passing of Dr. APJ Abdul Kalam, Dr. Pillai decided to leave the business and dedicate himself to reading, studying, researching, and experimenting.

During his tenure in the export business, Dr. Pillai traveled to over 16 countries, gaining valuable insight and experiencing the world and life in detail.

Dr. Pillai has achieved four Guinness World Records in the following subjects:

"Script to Screen" - In this record, Dr. Pillai produced and directed an animation film within the shortest time possible, breaking the previous record set by Canadians. He has also received numerous national and international awards and recognitions for this achievement.

Longest Line of Postcards - For this record, Dr. Pillai created a line of 16,300 postcards on the occasion of the 163rd anniversary of Indian Postal Day. The event also included a questionnaire about the Indian flag.

Largest Poster Awareness Campaign - Dr. Pillai designed an awareness campaign on the subject of "Beti Bachao - Beti Padhao" (Save the Girl Child - Educate the Girl Child) to achieve this record.

Largest Envelope - In tribute to the Indian Prime Minister's "Make in India" initiative, Dr. Pillai created a 4000 square meter envelope using waste paper to achieve this record.

Attempted - **70000 Candles on a 210 kg Cake** - To celebrate the 70th Indian Independence Day, Dr. Pillai attempted to light 70,000 candles on a 210 kg cake, which was recorded in World Records India.

Attempted - **Documentary on Dhamek Stupa of Sarnath in 17 Languages** - Dr. Pillai attempted to create a documentary on the Dhamek Stupa of Sarnath, dubbing it in 17 different languages. The result of this attempt is currently awaiting confirmation from the Guinness World Records.

Dr. Pillai is skilled in teaching the Bhagavad Gita, a Hindu scripture, and is popular among young people. He has helped many young people improve their lives through his motivational teachings.

In addition to teaching, he has composed and sung numerous Sanskrit Bhajans and patriotic songs.

He has also written and directed several short films and documentaries for awareness campaigns, and has volunteered with the police in both UP and Kerala to spread awareness about various issues through videos and photography.

Incredibly, he has produced and directed over 100 documentaries about the city of Varanasi, all on his own.

He has also helped and guided more than 25 boys and girls to achieve world records through creative and innovative methods. He is a multifaceted person who uses his intellect and the blessings given to him by God to excel in various areas. He is both a teacher and a student, always learning and teaching, and is able to master any subject he comes across.

He is a selfless social activist and motivational speaker who has overcome struggles and failures to become a successful and enthusiastic individual with a rich life experience.

In addition to his work with the Bhagavad Gita, he is also an efficient Tarot card reader, Astro-Vastu consultant, and a talented singer and composer. He has sung the entire Ram Charita Manas and Bhagavad Gita in his own compositions, and has sung the phrase "Lokah Samastha Sukhino Bhavantu" in 50 different languages. He is currently working on a detailed and scientific study of Vedas, Upanishads, Puranas, and the Bhagavad Gita. He has also composed and sung the Hanuman Chalisa and Gayatri Mantra in 108 and 1008 different compositions, respectively.

Awards - Four Times Guinness World Records, Winner of Mahatma Gandhi Vishwa Shanti Puraskar, Mahatma Gandhi Global Peace Ambassador, Kashi Ratna Award, Dr. APJ Abdul Kalam Motivational Person of the Year 2017, Mother Teresa Award, Indira Gandhi Priyadarshini Award, Bharat Vikas Ratna Award, Udyog Ratna Award, Vigyan Prasar Award, Poorvanchal Ratn Samman.

PREFACE

India is renowned for its rich and vibrant culture, and its street performances are no exception. This book, The Indian Street Performances: A Cultural Exploration of India's Street Performances, seeks to explore the culture, art, and tradition behind India's street performances.

This book is intended to serve as an introduction to the rich history and culture of Indian street performances for readers who are new to the subject. It explores the art of street performance in India, street performance as a cultural expression, street performance and social inclusion, street performance and social change, street performance and empowerment, street performance and identity, street performance and storytelling, street performance and music, and street performance and dance.

The book draws on research from a variety of sources, including interviews with key figures in the Indian street performance industry, archival materials, and cultural analysis. I have also conducted extensive field research in India, including attending festivals, interviewing street performers, and visiting locations associated with the production of street performances. Through this research, I hope to provide readers with a comprehensive understanding of the Indian street performance industry and its various components.

I am deeply passionate about the art of Indian street performances and hope that this book will help to spread the appreciation of this wonderful form of cultural expression. I believe that Indian street performances have a great deal to offer to the world and I am excited to share their cultural and historical significance with my readers.

I

Introduction to Indian Street Performances

India is a land of diverse cultures and traditions, and nowhere is this diversity more evident than in the country's street performances. From the bustling streets of Mumbai to the small villages of rural India, street performances have long been an integral part of the country's cultural landscape. These performances, which range from music and dance to puppetry and acrobatics, offer a unique glimpse into the rich tapestry of Indian culture.

Street performances in India can be traced back to ancient times, when wandering bards and minstrels would travel from village to village, entertaining the local people with stories, songs, and dances. Over the centuries, these performances have evolved to include a wide range of acts, from traditional forms such as Kathakali and Ramlila to more contemporary acts like breakdancing and hip-hop.

One of the most popular forms of street performance in India is the "Jatra" or "Yatra" which is a traditional form of rural theatre. These performances, which are usually held in open-air stages, feature a mix of music, dance, and drama, and are often based on religious themes or local legends.

Another popular form of street performance in India is "Kathputli" which is a form of puppetry, performed mainly in Rajasthan. These performances feature intricate wooden puppets, which are manipulated by skilled puppeteers, and tell stories of kings, queens, and other characters from Indian mythology.

In addition to these traditional forms of street performance, India is also home to a vibrant and growing contemporary street performance scene. From buskers and street performers in the major cities to community-based performance groups in rural areas, these acts often blend traditional and contemporary forms, to create a unique and dynamic performance.

Despite the rich tradition of street performances in India, the art form has been facing challenges in recent years. From a lack of funding to a lack of venues and audiences, street performers often struggle to make a living. However, there are also efforts to preserve and promote street performances, with government and private initiatives working to support the artists and provide them with the resources they need to continue performing.

Overall, Indian street performances offer a window into the country's rich cultural heritage, and provide a glimpse into the lives and traditions of the people who call India home. Whether you are a traveler looking to experience something new or a local looking to reconnect with your roots, the Indian street performances are a must-see experience.

"Street performances are the heartbeat of India's culture, pulsing with energy and tradition."

৪৩

II

The Art of Street Performance in India

Street performances, also known as "street theatre," have been a vital part of Indian culture for centuries. They are a unique form of art that combines music, dance, and drama to entertain and engage audiences in public spaces. These performances are not only a source of entertainment, but they also play an important role in preserving and promoting traditional Indian culture.

In India, street performances can be found in a variety of forms, including puppetry, magic shows, acrobatics, and traditional dance and music performances. These performances are often found in crowded marketplaces, street corners, and other public spaces, where audiences can gather to watch and enjoy the show.

One of the most popular forms of street performance in India is puppetry. Puppetry is a traditional art form that has been passed down through generations. Puppeteers use colorful and intricately designed puppets to tell stories and convey messages. These performances are often accompanied by music and narration, and are a favorite among both children and adults.

Another popular form of street performance in India is the "Jatra" performance. Jatra is a traditional form of theater that originated in Bengal. These performances are often held in open-air theaters and feature live music, dance, and drama. They often depict stories from Indian mythology and are a celebration of traditional Indian culture.

Magic shows are also a popular form of street performance in India. These performances feature illusions and other magical acts, and are often accompanied by music and narration. Street magicians in India often use traditional Indian props and techniques, such as the Indian Rope Trick, to entertain their audiences.

Acrobatics is yet another form of street performance that is popular in India. These performances feature acrobats performing death-defying stunts and other feats of physical prowess. These performances are often accompanied by music and narration, and are a favorite among audiences of all ages.

Overall, street performances in India offer a unique and exciting way to experience traditional Indian culture. They are a vibrant and colorful part of Indian society and are a testament to the country's rich artistic heritage.

DR. JAGADEESH PILLAI

*"Through street performances, we can see the
soul of India come alive."*

క్ర

III

Street Performance as a Cultural Expression

Street performances in India have been a rich part of the country's cultural heritage for centuries. From traditional dance and music performances to acrobatics and magic shows, street performers have captivated audiences with their skill and artistry. These performances are not just a form of entertainment, but also serve as a means of expression and storytelling, showcasing the diverse customs and traditions of India's various regions.

One of the most popular forms of street performance in India is traditional dance and music. These performances often feature vibrant costumes and intricate choreography, and are a celebration of India's rich cultural heritage. From the classical Kathak dance of North India to the Bhangra folk dance of Punjab, these performances offer a glimpse into the diverse customs and traditions of India's different regions.

Another popular form of street performance in India is acrobatics and magic shows. These performances feature skilled performers who amaze audiences with their agility and dexterity, performing stunts and tricks that are both entertaining and awe-inspiring. These performances often include elements of Indian mythology and folklore, making them an important part of the country's cultural heritage.

In addition to traditional dance and music performances, street performers in India also include puppeteers, comedians, and storytellers. These performers use their art to entertain and educate audiences, sharing stories and messages that are both meaningful and relevant to their audience. Puppeteers, for example, often tell traditional stories from Indian mythology, while comedians and storytellers use humor and wit to engage their audience.

Overall, street performances in India are an important part of the country's cultural heritage, showcasing the diverse customs and traditions of its different regions. These performances are not just a form of entertainment, but also serve as a means of expression and storytelling, and are enjoyed by people of all ages and backgrounds. Whether you're a tourist or a local, experiencing a street performance in India is a must-do for anyone interested in the country's rich culture and heritage.

"Street performances are not just entertainment, they are a window into India's rich history and heritage."

৪৩

IV

Popular Street Performances in India

Street performances in India have been a part of the country's cultural fabric for centuries. From traditional dance and music performances to acrobatics and clown acts, street performers can be found in almost every major city and town in India. These performances are not just a source of entertainment, but also a way for performers to earn a livelihood and for communities to come together and share in the joy of the arts.

One of the most popular forms of street performance in India is the traditional dance and music performance. These performances often feature dancers dressed in colorful costumes, accompanied by live musicians playing traditional instruments. These performances are usually rooted in Indian folklore and mythology, and are a way for performers to share their cultural heritage with audiences.

Another popular form of street performance in India is acrobatics. From tightrope walkers to contortionists and jugglers, acrobatic performers can be found in many of India's major cities. These performances are often a source of amazement and wonder for audiences, and are a way for performers to showcase their skills and physical prowess.

Clown acts are also a common sight on the streets of India. These performers often use comedy and slapstick to entertain audiences, and are a popular choice for children's birthday parties and other celebrations.

Street performance not only provides entertainment but also a platform for marginalised communities, such as Dalits and tribals, to showcase their talents and earn a livelihood. It also helps to promote social inclusion and break down barriers between different communities.

In recent years, street performances have become an important part of India's cultural tourism industry, attracting visitors from around the world who are interested in experiencing the country's rich cultural heritage. With its diverse array of performances and its deep cultural roots, Indian street performance is a unique and fascinating art form that is well worth exploring.

"The art of street performance is a celebration
of India's diversity and creativity."

৪৩

V

Street Performers and their Significance in Indian Culture

Street performances have been an integral part of Indian culture for centuries. They are a reflection of the rich and diverse cultural heritage of the country, and a celebration of the arts and creativity of the Indian people. From the traditional puppet shows and acrobatic performances of the north to the vibrant and colorful street theater of the south, street performances in India offer a unique and immersive cultural experience for both locals and tourists alike.

The art of street performance in India is characterized by its diversity and spontaneity. It encompasses a wide range of forms, including music, dance, theater, magic, acrobatics, and more. Performers come from all backgrounds and walks of life, and they use their talents and skills to entertain, educate, and inspire audiences of all ages.

Street performance is also a powerful tool for cultural expression. It is a way for artists to communicate their stories and messages to the public, and to reflect on the social and political issues of the day. Street performers use their talents to raise awareness and promote social change, and they often use their performances as a way to challenge the status quo and to promote equality and justice.

Street performance is also an important tool for social inclusion. It provides a platform for marginalized and underrepresented groups to share their stories and perspectives with a wider audience. Street performers often come from disadvantaged backgrounds, and their performances help to break down barriers and to promote understanding and acceptance.

Overall, street performances in India are an essential part of the country's cultural heritage. They offer a unique and immersive experience for locals and tourists alike, and they provide a powerful tool for cultural expression, social inclusion, and social change.

"Street performances are a powerful tool for preserving and promoting Indian culture."

છ

VI

Popular Forms of Street Performance in India

Throughout India, there are a variety of street performances that can be seen on the streets, from traditional dances and music to acrobatics and puppetry. Some of the most popular forms of street performance in India include:

Kathakali: This is a traditional dance-drama form from the Indian state of Kerala, characterized by elaborate make-up, costumes and gestures.

Kalarippayattu: This is a martial art form from the state of Kerala, which is also performed as a street performance.

Bhavai: This is a traditional folk theatre form from the Indian state of Gujarat, where the performers balance multiple earthen pots or other objects on their heads while dancing.

Jatra: This is a traditional folk theatre form from the Indian states of West Bengal and Orissa, which is performed on open-air stages and is known for its elaborate costumes, music, and dance.

Chhau: This is a traditional dance form from the Indian states of West Bengal, Jharkhand, and Odisha, which is characterized by its acrobatic movements and masks.

Bhangra: This is a popular folk dance form from the Indian state of Punjab, which is known for its energetic movements and beats.

Yakshagana: This is a traditional theater form from the Indian state of Karnataka, which is known for its elaborate costumes and make-up, as well as its use of music and dance.

Dharohar: This is a traditional dance form from the Indian state of Rajasthan, which is characterized by its colorful costumes and use of traditional instruments such as the dhol and sarangi.

Tamasha: This is a traditional theater form from the Indian state of Maharashtra, which is known for its use of music and dance, as well as its colorful costumes.

Ramlila: This is a traditional form of street theater in which the life of Lord Rama is enacted, performed mainly in the northern parts of India.

Nautanki: This is a popular form of street theater in northern India, which is known for its use of music, dance, and satire.

Shadow puppetry: This is a traditional form of street theater that is performed using puppets made of leather and is particularly popular in southern India.

Magic shows: This is a traditional form of street entertainment that is popular in many parts of India, featuring magicians performing illusions and tricks.

Street Musicians and performers: Street musicians and performers are a common sight on the streets of India, performing everything from traditional folk songs to contemporary music.

Street painters and portrait artists: Many Indian streets are adorned with the work of street painters and portrait artists, who can be seen creating detailed and colorful works of art on the spot.

"Street performances are not just a source of entertainment, but a means of expression and empowerment."

VII

Street Performance and its Impact on Tourism

Street performances in India have been a significant part of the country's cultural heritage for centuries. They are an integral part of the country's rich art and culture, and are an expression of the vibrant and diverse society that India is. Street performances in India are a reflection of the country's history and its people. They are an important part of the country's cultural identity and heritage.

Street performances in India are a form of artistic expression that reflects the society's values, beliefs, and customs. They are a medium through which the performers can express their creativity and showcase their talents. Street performances are also an opportunity for the performers to connect with the audience, to share their emotions and to tell their stories.

Street performances in India also play an important role in promoting social inclusion. They provide a platform for marginalized communities and underprivileged groups to showcase their talents and to be recognized for their contributions to the society. Street performances can also be a powerful tool for social change, as they can raise awareness about important social issues and inspire people to take action.

Street performances in India also play an important role in empowering the performers. They provide them with an opportunity to earn a livelihood, to be independent, and to be recognized for their talents. Street performances are also an important part of the performer's identity, as it is an expression of who they are and what they stand for.

Street performances also have a significant impact on tourism in India. They attract a lot of tourists from all over the world, who come to witness the country's rich culture and heritage. Street performances are a unique and authentic way for tourists to experience India's art and culture. They provide a platform for tourists to connect with the local community and to learn about the country's customs and traditions.

In conclusion, street performances in India are an essential part of the country's rich cultural heritage. They are a reflection of the country's history, its people, and its values. Street performances are a medium through which the performers can express their creativity, connect with the audience, and promote social inclusion, empowerment, and change. They also play an important role in promoting tourism in India and showcasing the country's rich culture and heritage to the world.

"For those who truly want to experience India, they must witness the magic of street performances."

ॐ

VIII

The Role of Street Performance in Indian Festivals and Celebrations

Street performance, also known as street theater or busking, has a rich history in India and is an integral part of the country's cultural landscape. It is a form of public performance that takes place on the streets, in markets, at festivals, and other public spaces. Street performers in India include musicians, dancers, magicians, acrobats, puppeteers, and more.

Street performance in India is not just entertainment, but also a cultural expression. It is a way for performers to showcase their talents and express their creativity. Street performances often reflect the local culture and traditions, and can be a window into the social and political issues of the time.

Street performance also plays an important role in social inclusion in India. It provides a platform for marginalized and underprivileged communities to showcase their talents and gain recognition. Street performers often come from marginalized backgrounds and use their performances as a means of empowerment and self-expression.

Street performance can also be a tool for social change. Performers often use their talents to raise awareness about important social and political issues, such as poverty, corruption, and discrimination. Through their performances, they can educate and inspire audiences to take action on these issues.

Street performance also plays an important role in the formation of identity. It provides a way for people to express their unique culture and tradition, and to connect with others who share a similar identity. Performances can also help preserve traditional art forms that might otherwise be lost.

Street performance is also closely tied to storytelling in India. Many street performers use storytelling as a way to convey messages and connect with audiences. They might use traditional stories, myths, or legends to entertain and educate audiences.

Street performance is also an integral part of Indian festivals and celebrations. It is a way for people to come together and celebrate the local culture and traditions. Street performers are often a highlight of festivals and celebrations, and their performances add to the festive atmosphere.

Overall, Indian street performances are an important part of the country's cultural heritage. They provide a platform for cultural expression, social inclusion, empowerment, and storytelling. They also play an important role in preserving traditional art forms and adding to the festive atmosphere of Indian celebrations.

"In India, street performances are a vital
component of the cultural fabric."

ℰ℘

IX

Street Performance and Dance: A Cultural Fusion

Street performance in India has been an integral part of the country's cultural expression for centuries. One of the most captivating forms of street performance in India is dance. From traditional classical dances to contemporary street styles, dance performances on the streets of India are a vibrant and dynamic display of the country's rich cultural heritage.

Dance performances on the streets of India are a fusion of traditional and contemporary styles. Classical dance forms such as Bharatanatyam, Kathak, and Kathakali are often performed alongside more modern styles such as B-boying and hip-hop. This fusion of styles creates a unique and dynamic display of Indian culture that is both familiar and fresh.

Street performance and dance also play an important role in social inclusion. Dance performances on the streets are often inclusive and open to all, regardless of social status or background. They provide a platform for marginalized communities to showcase their talents and express their identities. Street performance and dance also play an important role in social change, as they can be used to raise awareness of important social issues such as gender equality and education.

Street performance and dance also empower individuals and communities. Dancers on the streets of India often come from disadvantaged backgrounds and may not have had the opportunity to pursue formal dance training. Street performance provides them with a platform to showcase their talents and gain recognition for their skills.

Street performance and dance are also an important aspect of Indian identity. They provide a tangible connection to the country's cultural heritage and help to preserve traditional arts and practices. Street performance and dance also play an important role in storytelling, as they are often used to convey traditional myths, legends, and cultural stories.

In conclusion, street performance and dance are an essential part of India's cultural heritage and continue to play an important role in the country's cultural expression. They provide a platform for individuals and communities to express themselves, promote social inclusion, and empower marginalized communities. They also help to preserve traditional arts and practices, and contribute to the cultural richness of India.

"Street performances have the power to bring people together, breaking down barriers and fostering a sense of community."

ଞ୦

X

Street Performances and Traditional Arts

Street performances in India are a vibrant blend of traditional art forms and modern expressions. Dance is an integral part of Indian street performances, with various styles and forms being showcased on the streets. From classical dance forms such as Bharatanatyam and Kathak, to folk dances such as Bhangra and Garba, street performers showcase a wide range of dance styles.

One of the most popular street performances in India is the Kathakali dance-drama, which is a traditional art form from the state of Kerala. This dance form is characterized by elaborate costumes, face paint, and intricate hand gestures. Street performers also showcase various other traditional dance forms such as Kathak and Odissi, which are steeped in history and culture.

Folk dances are also a common sight in Indian street performances. Bhangra, a lively dance form from the state of Punjab, is performed with great energy and enthusiasm by street performers. Similarly, Garba, a traditional dance form from Gujarat, is performed with great passion and vigor. These dances are usually performed in a group, and the performers are dressed in traditional attire, adding to the cultural essence of the performance.

In addition to traditional dance forms, street performers also showcase contemporary dance styles such as hip-hop and b-boying. These performances are a fusion of traditional and modern elements, and showcase the diversity of Indian street performances.

In conclusion, street performances in India are a showcase of the country's rich cultural heritage and diversity. Dance is an integral part of these performances, and the various dance styles and forms showcased on the streets are a reflection of India's cultural richness. From traditional dance forms to contemporary styles, street performances in India offer a glimpse into the country's rich cultural heritage.

"Street performances are a reflection of
India's vibrant and colorful society."

&

XI

The Importance of Street Performances in Indian Culture.

Street performances in India are an integral part of the country's rich cultural heritage. They are a vibrant and dynamic form of expression, showcasing the diversity and richness of Indian culture. From dance and music to storytelling and traditional arts, street performances offer a glimpse into the daily life and customs of the Indian people. They are a reflection of the country's history, its people and its culture. Street performances are also an important source of income for many performers, who rely on the support of their communities to survive.

They are an important way to preserve and promote traditional arts, and to keep alive the cultural heritage of

India. In addition, street performances also play a significant role in tourism, as they attract visitors from around the world to experience the richness of Indian culture.

With the rapid modernization of the country, it is important to preserve and promote street performances, so that future generations can continue to experience and appreciate the unique beauty and diversity of Indian culture.

"The beauty of street performances lies in their ability to tell stories and convey emotions in a unique and powerful way."

৪৩

XII

Street Performances and Traditional Arts

Street Performance and Dance is an integral part of Indian culture and tradition. From the vibrant and colorful Kathak to the graceful and fluid Bharatanatyam, Indian street performances showcase the rich and diverse dance forms of the country.

Street performances of dance have been a part of Indian culture for centuries and have evolved to become an important aspect of the country's cultural heritage. These performances are typically performed by local communities and are usually accompanied by live music. The dancers often wear traditional costumes and use traditional props to enhance the performance.

The traditional dance forms such as Kathak,

Bharatanatyam, and Kathakali are typically performed in temples and other sacred spaces, while the more contemporary forms such as Bollywood-style dancing are performed in public spaces such as streets and parks.

Street performances of dance are not only a source of entertainment but also a means of preserving and promoting traditional arts. These performances are often organized by local cultural organizations and are an important source of income for the performers.

Street performances of dance also play an important role in promoting social inclusion and empowerment. They provide a platform for marginalized communities to showcase their talents and skills, and to express themselves creatively.

In addition to traditional dance forms, street performances in India also include other forms of dance such as folk dance and contemporary dance. These performances are a reflection of the country's diverse cultural and artistic traditions and offer a glimpse into the rich heritage of India.

In conclusion, street performances of dance in India are a vibrant and dynamic aspect of the country's culture and tradition. These performances showcase the rich and diverse dance forms of India, and play an important role in preserving and promoting traditional arts, promoting social inclusion and empowerment, and providing a platform for marginalized communities to express themselves creatively.

DR. JAGADEESH PILLAI

*"Street performances are a celebration of
India's rich musical heritage."*

&

XIII

Street Performances and the Preservation of Cultural Heritage

Street performances are a vital aspect of India's cultural heritage, and they play a significant role in preserving traditional arts and practices. Many traditional performances, such as classical dance and music, are passed down through generations of performers, and street performances provide a platform for these art forms to be shared with new audiences. By showcasing these traditional performances on the streets, performers are able to keep the art alive and ensure that it is not lost to time.

In addition to preserving traditional art forms, street performances also play a role in the tourism industry in

India. Tourists are often drawn to the vibrant and diverse street performance scene, and it can be a major draw for visitors to a particular city or region. Street performances can provide a unique insight into local culture and traditions, and they can be a memorable and enriching experience for tourists.

Overall, street performances in India play a crucial role in preserving cultural heritage, promoting social inclusion and change, and promoting the tourism industry. As a form of cultural expression, street performances are an integral part of Indian society and a window into the country's rich and diverse cultural heritage.

"Street performances are a vital part of
India's tourism industry, showcasing the
country's culture and traditions to the
world."

છ

XIV

Preserving and Promoting Street Performances

Street performances are an important part of India's cultural heritage, and preserving and promoting these performances is crucial for ensuring their continued existence. One way to preserve and promote street performances is through documentation and research. This can include collecting information about the performers, their performances, and their cultural significance. Another way to preserve and promote street performances is through education and awareness. This can include educating the public about the value and importance of street performances, and promoting opportunities for people to experience and appreciate these performances.

Another way to preserve and promote street performances is through partnerships and collaborations between local communities, government agencies, and private organizations. These partnerships can help to provide resources and support for street performers, and can also help to raise awareness and promote these performances to a wider audience. Additionally, it is important for street performers to be recognized and compensated for their work. This can include providing financial support for performers, as well as providing opportunities for them to showcase their talents to larger audiences.

Ultimately, preserving and promoting street performances is about valuing and celebrating the cultural heritage of India, and the unique and vibrant traditions that are embodied in these performances. By working together, we can ensure that these traditions continue to be passed down from generation to generation, and that future generations will have the opportunity to experience and appreciate the beauty and richness of Indian street performances.

*"Street performances are a reminder of the
richness and depth of Indian culture and a
celebration of the human spirit."*

&

XV

The Future of Street Performances in India

Street Performances in India are a unique and vibrant aspect of the country's culture that has been an integral part of the Indian society for centuries. The dynamic and diverse nature of street performances in India reflects the country's rich cultural heritage, social and economic diversity, and its ability to adapt to change. Street performances are not just forms of entertainment but also serve as powerful mediums of expression, social inclusion, empowerment, and identity. It is essential that we acknowledge and celebrate the cultural significance of street performances in India and work towards preserving and promoting them for future generations to enjoy.

● 72 ●

"Street performances are a treasure to be preserved and passed on to future generations."

୫୬

Other Books Of The Author

CONTACT

DR. JAGADEESH PILLAI

MBA & PhD in Vedic Science

Four Times Guinness World Record Holder

Winner of Mahatma Gandhi Vishwa Shanti Puraskar and
Global Peace Ambassador

Gemology, Astro & Vastu Consultant - Spiritual Counselor

Consultant for designing World Record Ideas

Efficient Tarot Card Reader

9839093003

myrichindia@gmail.com

drjagadeeshpillai@facebook

drjagadeeshpillai@instagram
jagadeeshpillai@youtube

www. JAGADEESHPILLAI.com

|| LOKAHA SAMASTHAHA SUKHINO BHAVANTU ||